W9-BTL-506

## word building

# Caring for Pets

## Word Building with Prefixes and Suffixes

**Pam Scheunemann**

Consulting Editor, Diane Craig, M.A./Reading Specialist

A Division of ABDO

**ABDO**
Publishing Company

# visit us at www.abdopublishing.com

Published by ABDO Publishing Company, a division of ABDO, P.O. Box 398166, Minneapolis, Minnesota 55439. Copyright © 2013 by Abdo Consulting Group, Inc. International copyrights reserved in all countries. No part of this book may be reproduced in any form without written permission from the publisher. Super SandCastle™ is a trademark and logo of ABDO Publishing Company.

Printed in the United States of America, North Mankato, Minnesota
062012
092012

 PRINTED ON RECYCLED PAPER

Editor: Liz Salzmann
Content Developer: Nancy Tuminelly
Interior Design: Kelly Doudna, Mighty Media, Inc.
Production: Oona Gaarder-Juntti, Mighty Media, Inc.
Photo Credits: Brand X pictures, Digital Vision, John Howard, Jupiterimages, Maria Teijeiro, Ryan McVay, Shutterstock, Steven Wewerka, Wewerka Photography

**Library of Congress Cataloging-in-Publication Data**
Scheunemann, Pam, 1955-
  Caring for Pets : word building with prefixes and suffixes / Pam Scheunemann.
       p. cm. --  (Word building)
  ISBN 978-1-61714-970-2
  1.  English language--Suffixes and prefixes--Juvenile literature. 2.  Vocabulary--Juvenile literature. 3.  Language arts (Elementary)  I. Title.
  PE1175.S33 2012
  428.1--dc22
                                    2010054481

Super SandCastle™ books are created by a team of professional educators, reading specialists, and content developers around five essential components—phonemic awareness, phonics, vocabulary, text comprehension, and fluency—to assist young readers as they develop reading skills and strategies and increase their general knowledge. All books are written, reviewed, and leveled for guided reading, early reading intervention, and Accelerated Reader® programs for use in shared, guided, and independent reading and writing activities to support a balanced approach to literacy instruction.

# contents

# What is Word Building?

Word building is adding groups of letters to a word. The added letters change the word's meaning.

**trains**

# Prefix

Some groups of letters are added to the beginning of words. They are called prefixes. Some prefixes have more than one meaning.

# Suffix

Some groups of letters are added to the end of words. They are called suffixes. Some suffixes have more than one meaning.

## re + train + ed

prefix + base word + suffix

## retrained

The prefix **re** means to do it again.
The base word **train** means to teach an animal to obey.
The suffix **ed** means that the action already happened.
**Retrained** means someone already taught an animal to obey again.

# Let's Build Words

## wash

Sammy is waiting for someone to wash him.

Duke is unwashed.

6

Shannon and Mia are washing their dogs.

**unwashed**

The prefix **un** means not or opposite.

The suffix **ed** turns a word into an adjective.

**washing**

The suffix **ing** means that the action is happening now.

## More Words

washes, washer, rewash, rewashes, rewashing, washed

# name

Ethan is thinking of a name for his turtle.

Terri wants to rename her cat Speckles.

Alexis named her snake Velvet.

### re**name**

The prefix **re** means to do it again.

### nam**ed**

The suffix **ed** means that the action already happened.

## More Words

names, renames, naming, renaming, unnamed, nameless, namelessly, namelessness

## ❧ ❧ ❧ Rule ❧ ❧ ❧

When a verb ends with *e*, drop the *e* before adding **ed**.

# play

Dan likes to play with his hamster.

Fluffy is playing with a toy.

**play**ing

The suffix **ing** means that the action is happening now.

**re**play**s**

The prefix **re** means to do something again.

The suffix **s** means that the action is happening now.

## More Words

plays, played, player, players, replay, replaying

Elizabeth replays the movie of her dog Missy.

# friend

Toby the cat is Julia's best friend.

Bowser and Buddy are acting unfriendly to each other.

12

Tulip is one of Hayden's friends.

**unfriendly**

The prefix **un** means not or opposite.

The suffix **ly** turns a noun into an adjective.

**friends**

The suffix **s** means there is more than one.

## More Words

friendly, friendlier, friendliest, unfriendliest, friendship

13

# feed

Maria knows she should
feed her rabbit every day.

Lilly feeds
her rooster.

Eva is feeding a sheep.

**feeds**

The suffix **s** means that the action is happening now.

**feeding**

The suffix **ing** means that the action is happening now.

## More words

feeder, feeders, feedable, refeed, refeeding, unfeedable, refeeds

# Silky Is the Luckiest Cat!

fa la la

Blueberry Street

Silky the cat lives on Blueberry Street.

He likes living with Sarah. She's really sweet!

Sarah plays with Silky all day long.

And while they play, she sings a silly song.

Sarah brushes Silky until the tangles are gone.

Then she rebrushes him out on the lawn.

After playing and brushing, it's time to eat.

Silky loves eating, but he's not very neat!

Sarah pets Silky's tummy and his soft head.
She keeps petting him while she tucks him in bed.
Silky raises his paw to give Sarah a pat.
She gives him everything he needs. He's the luckiest cat!

# Match It Up!

Choose the word with the correct prefix or suffix to complete each sentence.

**1** The dogs like being _____.
   a. washing
   b. washed

**2** Joe is _____ his frog Hoppy.
   a. renaming
   b. names

**3** Rusty _____ in the mud.

    a. plays

    b. playing

**4** Charlie is being _____.

    a. unfriendly

    b. friendliest

**5** Hallie _____ greens to her rabbit.

    a. feeding

    b. feeds

# Glossary

**adjective** (pp. 7, 13) – a word used to describe someone or something. Tall, green, round, happy, and cold are all adjectives.

**change** (p. 4) – to alter or make different.

**lawn** (p. 18) – an area of grass around a house or other building.

**meaning** (pp. 4, 5) – the idea or sense of something said or written.

**noun** (p. 13) – a word that is the name of a person, place, or thing.

**opposite** (pp. 7, 13) – being completely different from another thing.

**tangle** (p. 18) – hair that is twisted or knotted together.

**verb** (p. 9) – a word for an action. Be, do, think, play, and sleep are all verbs.